Bees
and
Other Pollinators

Wendy Einstein
Einstein Sisters

KidsWorld

What is Pollination?

Pollen is a powdery dust. It is made in the female part of a flower, called the anther.

Flowering plants need to be pollinated to produce seeds and fruit. This means pollen from the male part of a plant must touch the female part of the same type of plant.

For some plants their pollen is carried by the wind to the next plant.

Some plants, like corn, rice and dandelions, can use their own pollen to self-pollinate. Most plants need pollen from another plant.

Most plants need other creatures to move the pollen from one plant to the next. These creatures are known as pollinators.

Many of our favorite foods, like apples, strawberries, almonds and cucumber, need bees to pollinate them.

Bees as Pollinators

Bees live on all continents except Antarctica. These insects live in many different habitats, from forests and grasslands to deserts and even Arctic tundra.

About 25,000 bee species live in the world. Some 4000 species live in North America, with about 800 species in Canada.

Bees are most active during the day, but a few species fly only at dusk and dawn. Some tropical bees even fly at night.

How Does it Work?

A bee's main food is nectar. As it walks around on a flower looking for nectar, pollen sticks to its body.

When the bee flies to the next flower to look for nectar, some of the pollen from the first flower falls off its body onto the stigma. The stigma is the male part of the flower.

When pollen from one flower sticks to the stigma of different flower from the same kind of plant, the flower is pollinated.

The Honeybee

Bees have 5 eyes —2 big eyes and 3 small eyes. The big eyes are called compound eyes and are made up of many tiny eyes. The small eyes are called ocelli. They see only light and movement.

A bee's tongue is called a proboscis. It is a long tube that acts like a straw so the bee can drink nectar. When it is not being used, the proboscis rolls up under the bee's face.

Honeybees and bumblebees have "pollen baskets" on their back legs. They store the pollen in these baskets to take back to the hive or nest.

Bees have 2 stomachs. One is for food, and the other is used to carry nectar back to the hive.

The honeybee has a hook on the end of its stinger. When it stings, the hook gets stuck in whatever was stung and gets torn off the bee's body. This is why honeybees can sting only once.

The Hive

Honeybees are not a North American species. Early settlers from Europe brought the bees to Canada and the U.S. almost 400 years ago so they could have honey.

Wild honeybees nest in holes of trees or cracks in rocks. Their homes are called nests, not hives.

Bees build honeycombs inside their nests. Honeycombs are made from wax, which comes from the bees' bodies. Each space in the honeycomb is called a cell.

Some cells are used for storing honey and pollen. The queen bee lays her eggs in other cells. The baby bees stay in the cells until they are fully grown.

Domestic bees build their nests in special boxes called hives. The beekeeper pulls the frames out of the box to collect the honey.

Worker Bees

A bee nest or hive is made up of 3 types of bees: worker bees, drones and the queen.

Worker bees have many jobs. The jobs they do change as the bees get older.

Most of the bees are worker bees. These are female bees that do not lay eggs.

New adult worker bees build the honeycomb and take care of the queen and the young bees.

When they are about 2 weeks old, they move pollen and nectar into cells. The nectar is turned into honey. The pollen is mixed with honey and fed to baby bees.

When they are about 3 weeks old, bees leave the nest to collect nectar and pollen, and bring it back to the hive.

Worker bees also guard the hive.

Queens and Drones

The queen is the biggest bee in the colony. She is almost twice the size of the worker bees.

The queen bee is the only bee in the hive that lays eggs. She can lay more than 2000 eggs per day.

Each hive only has 1 queen.

Drones are male bees. You can tell them apart from worker bees because they are larger and have larger eyes.

DRONE

Drones are the first eggs to hatch in the spring.

There are fewer drones than worker bees in a hive. They do not help take care of the hive or collect pollen, and nectar. Their only job is to mate with the queen.

Lifecycle

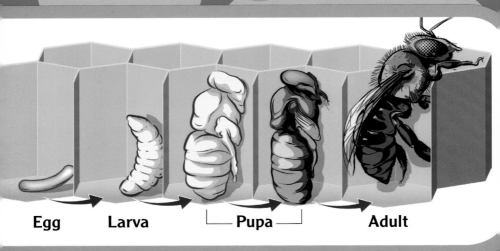

Egg → Larva → Pupa → Adult

Honeybees have 4 lifecycle stages: egg, larva, pupa and adult. It takes about 21 days for a bee to go from an egg to an adult.

Drones and worker bees live for about 6 weeks. Queens can live for 3 or 4 years.

An egg is about the same size as a grain of rice. Some eggs become female bees, others become drones.

Making Honey

The nectar a worker bee brings back to the hive is made into honey. Bees eat honey during winter when no flowers are in bloom. But how do they make it?

When the worker bee returns to the hive, she spits the nectar from her special stomach into the mouth of another worker bee.

The new bee spits it into another bee's mouth. This happens a few more times until the last bee spits it into a cell.

The bees then fan the nectar with their wings to evaporate the water. The nectar thickens into honey.

The worker bees cap the cells with wax to keep the honey safe.

Swarm!

When a honeybee colony gets too big, the queen and about half the worker bees leave the hive together to build a new nest. This big group of bees is called a swarm.

Because the queen is not a strong flyer, she finds a place to rest until scout bees find a place for the new nest. As she rests, most of the worker bees form a big ball around her to keep her safe.

When a colony
is planning to swarm,
many bees will gather at
the entrance to the nest
or hive. This behaviour
is called bearding.

Bees can also beard if
the hive gets too hot. The
bees at the entrance fan
their wings to cool
down the hive.

Cool Facts

Only female bees sting. Drones don't have stingers. If a bee is getting to close to you, don't swat it. Instead, blow gently on it, and the bee will fly away.

Bees can fly forward, backward and sideways. They can have trouble flying in the rain. If they get too cold, their wing muscles don't work well.

When a bee finds a good source of food, it does a "waggle dance" to tell other bees where to go. The direction the bee dances tells the others the direction to fly. The length of the dance tells the bees how far away the food source is from the hive.

Bees can see in colour but they can't see red. Their favorite colors of flowers are yellow, white, blue, violet and purple.

Bumblebees

If you see a huge fuzzy bee slowly flying past, it is probably a bumblebee.

Unlike honeybees, bumblebees do not die after they sting.

These fuzzy bees are not dangerous. If you leave them alone, they will not sting you. They sting only to protect themselves or their nest.

The buzzing noise a bumblebee makes shakes loose the pollen from inside the flowers. The pollen sticks to the bee's long hairs.

Because they are hairier than honeybees, bumblebees can forage in cooler temperatures. Some species can be found in the Arctic and Subarctic.

Bumblebee Colonies

Like honeybees, bumblebees are social bees that live in colonies. A bumblebee colony is much smaller than a honeybee colony. It has only a few hundred bees instead of thousands.

Bumblebees usually nest underground. They often use abandoned rodent nests. They will also nest in tall grass, under porches or behind steps.

Bumblebees live only 1 season. When winter comes, all the bees in the nest die except the newly hatched queens. These queens find a safe place to hibernate for the winter. In spring they build their own nests.

Solitary Bees

Most bee species are solitary. They live by themselves instead of in colonies with other bees.

There is no queen bee and no hive. Each female builds a nest to lay her eggs. Some species raise their young. Others leave after laying their eggs. The young bees take care of themselves.

Solitary bees are great pollinators. A lot of pollination is really done by solitary bees.

Many people do not notice solitary bees because many species don't look like regular bees. Some look like flies, and others look more like wasps.

Sweat bees are one common type of solitary bee.

Sweat Bees

They are called sweat bees because they will land on people's skin to lick their sweat. They like the salt in the sweat.

The many different species of sweat bee can be a metallic green, red or yellow. Some have bands like a honeybee.

Mason Bees

Mason bees nest in hollow stems or twigs. They are called mason bees because they use mud to close up their nests.

These small bees are sometimes compared to tiny fighter jets because they are such good fliers.

Mason bees can be a metallic green, black or blue colour.

Leafcutter bees are similar to mason bees, but they build their nests out of leaves.

The female bites small circles out of leaves and sticks them together with her spit to make a cocoon for her eggs. She stuffs another leaf into the end of the cocoon to seal it.

Leafcutter Bees

When they hatch, the baby bees eat their way out of the leaf cocoon.

Mining Bees

Mining bees are cute little bees that nest underground. They are solitary, but they often nest in the same area as other mining bees.

They are one of the main pollinators of blueberry bushes and apple trees.

These friendly little bees rarely sting.

Carpenter bees are big, like bumblebees. They look a lot like bumblebees, too, only with a bigger head and no hair on their abdomen.

Carpenter bees get their name from their habit of chewing holes in wood to make their nests.

Carpenter Bees

When is a Bee Not a Bee?

When it's a hoverfly!

A hoverfly looks a lot like a bee but it has huge eyes on the side of its head and only 2 wings instead of 4.

Hoverflies are great pollinators and can often be seen hovering near flowers.

These little flies have no stinger. They look and act like bees to protect themselves from predators.

Bees are not the only pollinators. Many other creatures are pollinators, too.

Butterflies collect less pollen than bees do, but they are still important pollinators. Pollen sticks to their legs and proboscis as they drink nectar.

Butterflies and Moths

Butterflies fly farther than bees do looking for nectar because they do not have a nest to go back to. Butterflies take pollen to plants far away from each other. This keeps the plants strong and healthy.

Moths are also important pollinators. Most pollinators are active during the day, but moths are active at night. They visit the plants that bloom at night.

Moths find the flowers by their scent instead of their color.

Beetles

Beetles are also
important pollinators,
especially in areas
where there are
few bees.

Most beetles
that visit plants do not
drink the nectar. They eat
the petals and other parts of
the flower. The pollen gets
stuck to their hard shell as
they move around in the
flowers.

Ladybugs **do eat nectar and pollen,** although their favorite food is aphids. **The female ladybug needs the nutrition from pollen and nectar to lay eggs.**

Soldier beetles are another type of common pollinating beetle. **Soldier beetle** larva are predators that eat other insects. The adults feed mostly on nectar and pollen.

Adult soldier beetles **can be** black, yellow **or** orange with black marks.

Hummingbirds

**Hummingbirds are one of the main
pollinators of wildflowers. Pollen sticks
to the birds' bill and forehead as they
hover by the plant to drink nectar.**

Hummingbirds are excellent fliers. They flap their wings so fast that they can hover in one place like a helicopter. They can also fly backwards or even upside down.

Bats

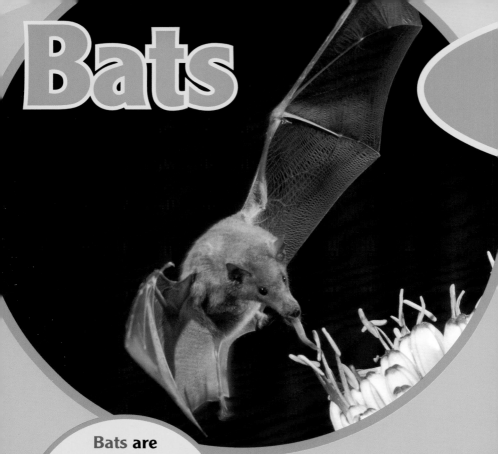

Bats are probably the most important mammal pollinator. They can fly long distances and visit many flowers in one night.

Not all bats are pollinators. Most bats eat insects or fruit. Only a few types of bats drink nectar and eat pollen. The pollen sticks in their fur as they drink nectar and is passed on to the next plant they visit.

Nectar bats have really long tongues. The Pallas' long-tongued bat's tongue is twice as long as its head. When the bat sticks its tongue into a flower, it fills with blood and little hairs on the end stand straight up. These hairs trap the nectar like a mop and let the bat scoop it out of the flower and into its mouth.

Bats pollinate more than 300 different kinds of plants, including bananas, avocadoes, dates, cashews and the cacao plant. Chocolate is made from the cacao plant. Without bats there would be no chocolate!!!!!

Ruffed Lemurs

In the wild, ruffed lemurs
live only on the island
of Madagascar. There are two types:
the black-and-white-ruffed lemur
and the red-ruffed lemur.

The black-and-white-ruffed lemur is the largest pollinator in the world.

Ruffed lemurs eat fruit, pollen and nectar. When they stick their long snout into flowers to get nectar, pollen sticks to their fur. When they stick their snout into the next flower, pollen from the first flower rubs off.

These lemurs are the only pollinators of the traveler's palm. They are the only creatures that can get the flowers open. This tree, like the lemurs, grows in the wild only in Madagascar.

The kinkajou lives in rainforests
of South America.

Kinkajou

The kinkajou
eats mostly fruit and
nectar. It pollinates
flowers as it goes
from plant to
plant drinking
nectar.

The kinkajou
is also known as
a seed disperser. This
means that it moves
a plant's seeds to
a different place, where
new plants can grow.

How does the kinkajou
disperse seeds? It eats
fruit from one tree,
walks to a different area
and poops. The seeds
pass out of its body in
its poo, and new plants
grow there.

The kinkajou can hold onto branches with its tail, like a monkey can. It often hangs from its tail to reach for fruit.

Sugar Glider

The sugar glider is a small possum that lives in Australia. It is most active at night.

The sugar glider eats mostly nectar and sap, as well as some insects.

The sugar glider lives in trees. It rarely, if ever, touches the ground.

To get from one place to the next the sugar glider jumps from a tree and spreads its front and back legs wide. Special flaps of skin, called patagium, connect its front legs to its back legs to act like a parachute, letting it glide safely from tree to tree.

All around the world, the number of pollinators is dropping. Some species, like kinkajous and beetles, are still common. But there are fewer species of butterfly and bees than ever.

Pollinators in Decline

As people tear up nature to build houses, shopping centres, roads and parking lots, there is less land for bees and butterflies. Pollinators have trouble finding the plants they need to eat and places to lay their eggs.

Ruffed lemurs are critically endangered. This means there are not many left in the wild. People keep cutting down the forests they need to survive.

Where are the Bees?

Bee populations worldwide are struggling. In North America, the number of solitary bees is much lower than it was only a few years ago.

Also, in the last few years, honeybees have been dying or disappearing. No one knows why.

When beekeepers go out to check their hives, many of the hives are empty. The worker bees have disappeared. Without worker bees to take care of them, the young bees and the queen die. The whole colony collapses. This problem has been named Colony Collapse Disorder.

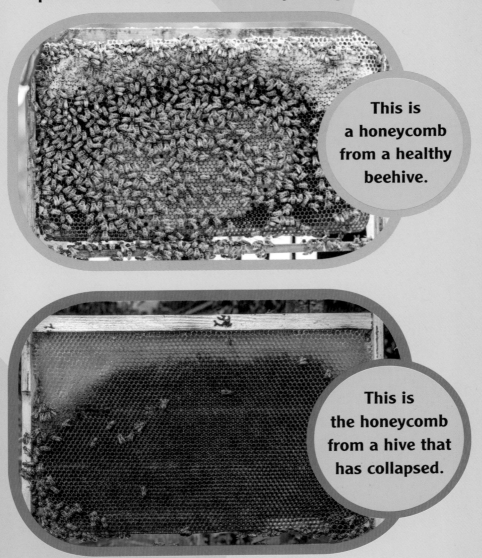

This is a honeycomb from a healthy beehive.

This is the honeycomb from a hive that has collapsed.

Monocultures

One of the biggest problems facing bees today is the way farmers grow their crops.

In the past, people grew their own food in smaller gardens. They planted many types of crops. This gave the bees many plants to visit to find nectar.

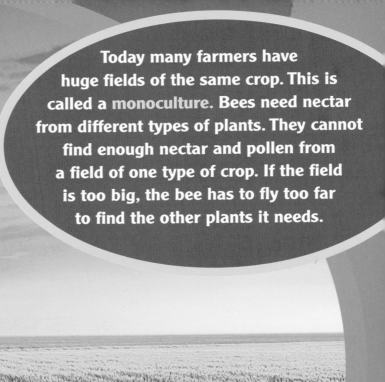

Today many farmers have huge fields of the same crop. This is called a monoculture. Bees need nectar from different types of plants. They cannot find enough nectar and pollen from a field of one type of crop. If the field is too big, the bee has to fly too far to find the other plants it needs.

Also, when a huge field of one crop is planted, it flowers at the same time. Once that crop stops flowering, there is no food for the bees. They need plants that flower at different times so they have a steady source of food.

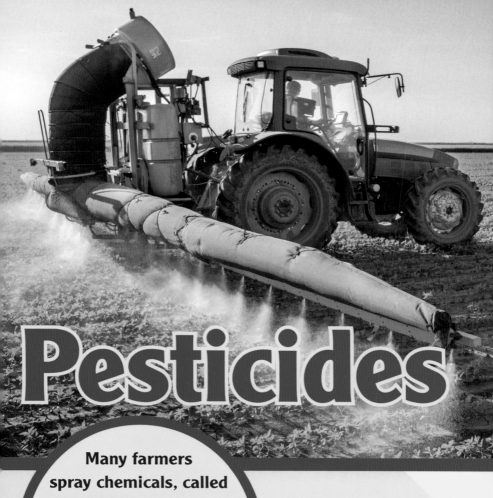

Pesticides

Many farmers spray chemicals, called pesticides, on their crops to protect them from bugs that could ruin the plants. These chemicals can also hurt bees.

Some of the pesticides kill the bees when they eat it or are sprayed with it. Other chemicals make the bees sick, so they have a shorter life.

Sometimes the pesticides change the bees' behaviour. The chemicals can confuse the bees so they can't forage for food or find their way back to the hive.

Some pesticides can also stop colonies from raising healthy baby bees. When the baby bees are fed pollen and nectar from plants sprayed with chemicals, they don't grow properly.

On the Move

On some farms, the fields of crops are so big that local bees cannot pollinate all the plants. To make sure their plants are pollinated, farmers rent beehives from beekeepers. This practice is called migratory beekeeping.

The beehives are loaded onto trucks and driven to a field that needs pollinating. Sometimes they travel long distances. Bees from southern Ontario can be taken all the way to California. The bees are locked in their hives while the hives are being moved.

Some researchers think migratory beekeeping is one of the reasons that bees are dying off.

Beekeepers feed their traveling bees sugar water instead of nectar or honey. The sugar water gives the bees energy, but it does not make them strong. Sugar does not give them the nutrition they need to be healthy. It would be the same as if you ate nothing but candy at every meal. You might not be hungry, but you wouldn't be healthy.

A World Without Bees

Bees are bioindicators. That means they can tell us if the environment is healthy or not. If bee populations are not doing well, the environment is not healthy.

Bees are also what is known as a keystone species. A keystone species is one that many other species depend on to survive.

Without bees, there would be fewer seeds and flowers. Other species, like birds and rodents, depend on seeds and flowers for their food. Bigger predators depend on the smaller animals for *their* food. Without bees, many animals would starve.

A lot of the food we eat, like strawberries, apples and cucumbers, depend on bees for pollination. Without bees, farmers would need to find other ways to pollinate their crops.

In China, some crops are pollinated by people. The people use paintbrushes to rub pollen on every plant. If there were no bees, farmers in North America would have to do the same thing.

If you want to help pollinators, plant a bee and butterfly garden. It doesn't have to be a big garden. It just has to have plants with different flowering times from spring to late fall.

Don't use pesticides or herbicides on your garden or lawn.

What Can You Do?

Give solitary bees a place to nest by setting up a bee hotel. You'll have to check it regularly to make sure other insects, like wasps, don't take it over.

Let your weeds grow until they finish flowering. Many people don't want dandelions on their lawn, but they are an important food source for bees before summer flowers start to bloom.

© 2018 KidsWorld Books
Printed in China

The Publisher: KidsWorld Books

Library and Archives Canada Cataloguing in Publication

Einstein, Wendy, author
  Bees and other pollinators / Wendy Einstein & Einstein Sisters.

ISBN 978-1-988183-38-1 (softcover)

  1. Bees--Juvenile literature. 2. Pollinators--Juvenile literature. 3. Pollination--Juvenile literature. I. Title.

QL565.2.E36 2018   j595.79'9   C2017-906846-6

Cover Images: Front cover: bigemrg/Thinkstock
Back cover: nnorozoff/Thinkstock; Shaiith/Thinkstock; luisbeluga/Thinkstock

Photo credits: From Thinkstock: abzerit, 36; akova, 7a; arinahabish, 21; BarbaraStorms, 29; bigemrg, 24; Biletskiy_Evgeniy, 54-55; BobMcLeanLLC, 33; buslig22, 35; ChezBriand, 41 ConstantinCornel, 8a; CreativeNature_nl, 60; DanielPrudek, 12; darios44, 18; diegograndi, 50; digitalg, 23a; dimarik, 9b; Dimijana, 6; fotokostic, 56; Freilajpg, 10b; Grisha Shoolepoff, 10a; HaiGala, 62; heibaihui, 14; HelenL100, 27, 39b; Henrik_L, 31; HPW, 3; jinga80, 57; John Foxx, 39a; Kamadie, 63b; KarenHBlack, 63a; kn1, 51; Kosala5, 23b; luisbeluga, 43; lukaves, 16; Nearchos, 48, 49; Neyya, 58; NinaHenry, 15; nnorozoff, 26; OK-photography, 53a; panom, 22; PaulGrecaud, 4; PaulJRobinson, 17b; Photografiero, 52, 53b; prill, 38; Prudek, 8b; Purestock, 37, 40; randimal, 30; RebeccaBloomPhoto, 42; sezer66, 5; Shaiith, 19; Sloot, 45; sommail, 20; stachu343, 17a; Steve_Hardiman, 2; StGrafix, 32; stockthor, 25; SumikoPhoto, 9a; thamerpic, 45a; Tom Brakefield, 46, 47; Valengilda, 13; VeselovaElena, 61; viktorkunz, 34; xalanx, 59; y-studio, 44; Zukovic, 11b; zwawol, 11a.

We acknowledge the financial support of the Government of Canada.
Nous reconnaissons l'appui financier du gouvernement du Canada.

Funded by the Government of Canada
Financé par le gouvernement du Canada | Canadä